Volume 110 of the Yale Series of Younger Poets

The Destroyer in the Glass

Noah Warren

Foreword by Carl Phillips

Yale UNIVERSITY PRESS

New Haven and London

Published with assistance from a grant to honor James Merrill and from the foundation established in memory of James Wesley Cooper of the Class of 1895, Yale College.

Yale University Press books may be purchased in quantity for educational, business, or promotional use. For information, please e-mail sales.press@ yale.edu (US office) or sales@yaleup.co.uk (UK office).

Designed by James J. Johnson.

Set in Apollo type by Westchester Publishing Services, Danbury, Connecticut.

Printed in the United States of America.

Library of Congress Control Number: 2015953455

ISBN 978-0-300-21714-8 (hardcover : alk. paper)

ISBN 978-0-300-21715-5 (paperbound : alk. paper)

A catalogue record for this book is available from the British Library.

This paper meets the requirements of ANSI/NISO Z39.48–1992 (Permanence of Paper).

10 9 8 7 6 5 4 3 2 1

I dedicate this book with love to
Ana, Gabriel, and Sofia.

I offer it to
Lucy.

Contents

Foreword

CARL PHILLIPS

There are many notes on which a new voice—its sensibility—
might announce itself; perhaps that of vertigo is not the worst
one. Noah Warren's *The Destroyer in the Glass* opens (not count-
ing, for now, the dedication poem, though I'll get to that) with
"Like the Pelican," a poem that resists parsing for what we usu-
ally seem to mean when we speak of meaning. The opening stanza
of the poem seems clear enough, until pushed against:

> The shape of the pelican
> swings back and forth
> across the mouth
> of the Cove of Now and Then.

A shape can indeed swing across the mouth of a cove, but why
does the shape here seem disconnected from the pelican? Not
the pelican, but its shape (not its shadow) swings across the
cove's mouth—how? And if the cove itself is not an actual
cove but an abstract one, the Cove of Now and Then? So we
have the shape of a thing—shape itself a form of abstraction—
passing across the mouth of an abstraction. And yet the sen-
tence that delivers this information sounds confident, as if
announcing some unassailable fact—a brief, direct sentence
that also takes the form of a closed, envelope (a-b-b-a rhyme)
stanza, a mirroring, at the level of sound, the sonic closure
adding to the stanza's authority, or at least the feel of it. That's
the poem's first sentence. The rest of the poem consists of a
single, ultimately undiagrammable sentence that stretches
across six stanzas. Part of what makes for the feeling of vertigo
is the sudden shift from the tightness of the first stanza (closed,
declarative) to the sprawl that takes over: not only are all the

stanzas open, enjambed (in meaningful tension with the fact that they, too, are envelope stanzas), but the poem itself ends without punctuation; meanwhile, not only does this six-stanza sentence let go of entirely clear syntax, the images inside the sentence swerve clear of easy connection—black notes, an ark, fingertips, the sea's lungs, two stars, eternity as choice and death, "all pity for the dying union," reefs of bone . . . . There's a sense at once of close observation of details and of being lost in, overwhelmed by, those details, all of it ending, though, in a clear-enough plea (if not prayer, exactly), not to the you who seems to have been lost sight of, but to the "dark water":

> trickle through my cells, my eyes, persist in me
> like the pelican
> that I may learn
> to see and not to see

Simultaneously seeing and not seeing—maybe that's what it means, to see the pelican's shape and not the pelican itself. Why long for this, though? Here, I find the dedicatory poem—cagily titled "To the Book (And Its Author)"—helpful, its ending, specifically:

> Swiftly, silently
> you fly from me.
> Still I fear you
>
> are not you
> except where
> you melt into air.

This idea of the self (the "you") as only being itself when it melts into air—that is, lacks actual substance—is telling. As with the desire to see only the shape of the pelican, not the substance around which a shape becomes possible, something seems to be getting said, here, about a fear of self-knowing, if to know the self is to understand the very substance—both physical and metaphysical—of which the self is made. The form of "Like the Pelican" enacts the tension between containment and sprawl, it lets us feel what that tug of war *feels* like, between the certainty of knowing and a willingness (and/or desire) to give in to disorientation, its wild *un*certainty. And I would suggest that the sensibility that governs this book as a whole has no choice but to live squarely inside that tension, as we watch the speaker shuttle back and forth between substance and an impulse away from it, sometimes "crouched like Samsa" ("New Vintage Stereo"), the man who famously lost his shape/identity in Franz Kafka's "The Metamorphosis," sometimes recalling the not-yet-filled-in nature of the body in boyhood ("the muscles were mere / ideas, tender, beautiful," from "The Tines"), or being twenty-two, that time when

> . . . . by exertion or hunger
> or sex or abject failure
> I could arrive at a state in which my body
> was hollowed out, leaving
> a skin which lived
> and seemed to see.

("On the Levee")

At other times, as in "The Problem Bear," there's on one hand a desire to find one's own substance in another's:

> It wasn't till we sawed the head
> off and peeled away the pelt
> that it became my body spread
> on the steel table, my muscles dark
> under a clear blue membrane, fist
> sized pockets of fat.

And there's a concomitant desire to destroy the found self as a way toward freedom:

But it took me straddling
the carcass and smashing down the raised ax
to break open the ribcage—

I seemed to walk through a door.

Seeking shape, eluding it; finding the self, only to destroy it; longing for that time, predisaster, when "The world was still, and it held / a measure of emptiness" ("A Beginning"), and yet realizing somewhere that that emptiness, the vestigial life, is more often only a distraction from the fact of substance, hard reality:

Walking so long, so slowly,

you become a vestige, a flaw
hidden in the long-exposure photograph—
as you desired—and you feel safe—

but your hands, pilgrim,
have twisted into claws of bone;
frantically you rub them; they only grate.

("Holt Hill")

Speaking of pilgrims: by that name, or by the name of tourist, there are many travelers in these poems; we find ourselves variously in Crete, Boston, New Orleans (city of masks and of shape-shifting if there ever was one), Helsingør (site of Kronborg Castle, the model for Hamlet's Elsinore), at the Winter Palace in Saint Petersburg . . . . Warren reminds us that travel is at least one means of, if only temporarily, escaping reality, we come to strangers with no apparent history—as we present our selves, we can also invent them. Travel is also, though, a form of communion, another tricky element in these poems. Throughout the book, I find an impulse toward communion with others as a way of, quite simply, not being utterly alone, even if that communion involves people who don't know we're there, as when the speaker of "Hopelessly Baroque, My Soul" hears the

neighbors playing the *Eroica,* seems half to envy them their
camaraderie, and in his own way joins in:

> I hoped that apartment was full of friends
> nestling together or sprawled on the floor
> with cups of cheap merlot, and some
> had closed their eyes for the funeral march
> and were humming along like me.

At other times, the sensibility is decidedly more insensitive, if
we can believe the account of a passing girlfriend:

> Or he would point questions: Was speaking
> as hard for me as it was for him?
> I had hurt; but had I hurt enough to speak?
>
> This last he mused in a cruelly even voice
> as I rode him: he refused to move with me
> and instead pinched hard the inside
> of my upper arm, then my ass, my full breast.

> ("A Bought Scene")

What communion requires is empathy, that ability to extend
oneself in such a way as to inhabit and know the self of another—
a difficult business for someone who has enough trouble with
self-knowing. As Warren puts it in "Thereafter," "To contain so
much empathy is hard—/ Aristotle knew what practice does to
you," referring to that place in the *Nichomachean Ethics* where
Aristotle says empathy is learnable, it just requires practice until
it becomes second nature. What Aristotle doesn't say, as far as I
know, but what Warren implies, is that empathy can be learned
to one's detriment. Empathy may at times save us from assuming
the world revolves around ourselves exclusively:

> I know I'm not the only one whose life is a conditional
> clause
>
> hanging from something to do with spring and one
> tall room and the tremble of my phone.

> I'm not the only one that love makes feel like a dozen
> flapping bedsheets being ripped to prayer flags by
> the wind.

("Cut Lilies")

But at other times the world—the self included—*can* be too
much with us, perhaps especially for the poet, constantly at
work trying to forge

> his forebrain to a lyre: some thing
> he can hold and have, that returns
> more life than it burns, a thing
> gorgeous, worthless, and self-betraying.

("Automatic Pool Cleaner")

At one point in *The Prelude,* Wordsworth describes his child
self as the "fell destroyer" of others' property; and he describes
his indifference to the damage he caused. I take *The Destroyer
in the Glass* to refer to the self as seen in the mirror, the po-
tential destroyer, equally, of others and of oneself. What to do
with that destructive capacity, which is finally also a form of
energy—which is to say, life—is indeed a question. Necessar-
ily, these are not poems of resolution, easy or otherwise. They
exist more committedly in that space of negative capability
than most poems I can think of, these days. Of course there can
be no "answer" to what it means—how to make meaning *from*
it—the particular difficulty of being human, self-conscious,
in a world of plants, animals—things—and of relative indif-
ference to the doomed and radiant facts of our passing selves.
"When I stand in full sun I feel I have been falling headfirst
for decades," Warren says early on in this book ("Cut Lilies");
it doesn't seem the best position to be in. Toward the end of
the book, though, falling seems more worth embracing than
resisting:

If my life is sad rich music,
very well—
may it fall upon the ear
drop by drop.

If I am tumbling from a high place,
may it last.

("On the Levee")

Resolution? Not quite. But honest—absolutely. There is confidence, here—even swagger, at times—but always tempered by a self-awareness that can be the catalyst for humility and, yes, empathy. Shakespeare speaks of glass doubling as mirror and as window. If Warren sees himself as the destroyer reflected in the mirror, he seems as well to see past that, I sense he sees me, too—I'd half forgotten that feeling, what only the highest art, in the end, provides.

To the Book (and Its Author)

I started you
from the cover
of an alder
four years ago.

I was walking
by the cold creek.
Perhaps you slept.

Swiftly, silently
you fly from me.
Still I fear you

are not you
except where
you melt into air

I

Like the Pelican

The shape of the pelican
swings back and forth
across the mouth
of the Cove of Now and Then.

So winter blooms, hot, stark—
three black notes,
you, me, *this,* float
together from the ark

revolving: wary we touch
fingertips and as our tongues
meet strung nerves thrum and the sea's lungs
boom our chord—a clutch

of heart in teeth—now hollower notes—
listen—
          shark rots on sand,
a breeze drains the land,
and two stars wink out

in rhythm—break open to theme and so prove eternity
is choice and death, choice—
love, its voice—
spread your gaze through my gaze, all pity

for the dying union, drown: this dark water
swallows planets,
dissolves the granite
cape, the reefs of bone—dark water

trickle through my cells, my eyes, persist in me
like the pelican
that I may learn
to see and not to see

After Du Fu

The bar he brought her to was green, loud, and they were
    both soft-spoken.
She said words he didn't hear, he nodded Yes—

When they left for the apartment, the streets had filled
    with snow.
She finished her point. His shoulders rose.

Black and red bangs hid half her face until on black ice
she fell, they whipped back, and, hurt, she cried.

I like you, she whispered, riding him, rocking back
and forth. But I'm seeing a lot of people right now. Her breast

grazed his face. He saw the streetlight irradiating
the window, slicing the cover, until he came. She made him
    leave,

and as he trudged green flames rose and flickered
in black windows, in the plow's swath, in the rigid river.

Cut Lilies

More than a hundred dollars of them.

It was pure folly. I had to find more glass things to stuff
    them in.

Now a white and purple cloud is breathing in each corner

of the room I love. Now a mass of flowers spills down my
    dining table—

each fresh-faced, extending delicate leaves

into the crush. Didn't I watch

children shuffle strictly in line, cradle

candles that dribbled hot white on their fingers,

chanting Latin—just to fashion Sevilla's Easter? Wasn't I sad?
    Didn't I use to

go mucking through streambeds with the skunk cabbage
    raising

bursting violet spears?—Look, the afternoon dies

as night begins in the heart of the lilies and smokes up

their fluted throats until it fills the room

and my lights have to be not switched on.

And in close darkness the aroma grows so sweet,

so strong, that it could slice me open. It does.

I know I'm not the only one whose life is a conditional clause

hanging from something to do with spring and one tall room
and the tremble of my phone.

I'm not the only one that love makes feel like a dozen

flapping bedsheets being ripped to prayer flags by the wind.

When I stand in full sun I feel I have been falling headfirst for
decades.

God, I am so transparent.

So light.

La Dolce Vita

Massachusetts and the remains
of winter dissolve like cream

into gray lawn, snarled alders,
and Rogers Brook. Two birdcalls

compete between the branches:
one fluent, descending, the other shrill.

While the water is so flexible, effortlessly
skirting rooted stones—

footage of a helicopter rising
in a widening helix above St. Peter's

was broadcast this morning:
I was told and would later read

that the Pope soared, in it, away, as Romans
thronged their balconies to watch.

Blank azure vaulted the immortal city; here,
ghostly brightness broke through, ten minutes at a time,

painted weird shadows, quickened the water;
a kiss for the fat vines, the spindly trunks.

Then dusk fumed from the lawn, and soon
two coin eyes glittered there, as if casing me—

my house, that is—I was invisible
behind the blind, wrapped in my thick blue robe.

2.28.2013
Benedict XVI

Thereafter

You had your sight, still, you saw the crane.
And you know you will remember it well.
Erect, white, his form wavered in its frame
when like a shadow in the wind came a lull.

You heard the tide's recession sucking
fire from the live mind of the flat.
Indifferently the crane is thrusting
his beak deep in the shallows of that.

To contain so much empathy is hard—
Aristotle knew what practice does to you.
In a flash, you've felt what you don't want to
without considering, or being on your guard.

You lecture the child on the dangers of the marsh.
He takes your hand or you his. You watch.

Holt Hill

December: the sap falls back
into the forest roots. The skeleton crew
crackles on the hill, in the wind.

When the soil has frozen
they'll fell the white pines. Their roads
are cut; like mantises, three huge *harvesters*

gleam beneath a shell of frost.
A livid moon rises; a screech owl threads
the scaled, swaying trees;

and drifts of shadow heap up
in the lee of an old stone wall.
Walking so long, so slowly,

you become a vestige, a flaw
hidden in the long-exposure photograph—
as you desired—and you feel safe—

but your hands, pilgrim,
have twisted into claws of bone;
frantically you rub them; they only grate.

New Vintage Stereo

Crouched like Samsa in the corner of my room,
dragging each half through the bladed tool,
I unseamed the last six inches of speaker wire.
The clear skin spilled a mess of copper veins.

I twisted the fanned filaments back together,
rolling them badly in my giant's fingertips.

I bent both ends to bright shepherds' crooks,
hooking each around its threaded column—
positive, red; ground, black—and turned
the golden screws until they crushed.

Two Apostrophes to the *Requiem*

Dies Irae

The Latin descends like a mace: *mox*
Mozart groans in his box, dreams
old roil, old crackle, the black anvil
head prostrate under hammer, its fall,
a ringing rumble, the thundercell
                                    fissuring apart:

lo, you storm from the shell.
You are the masque of hell

and the pike thereto—a swollen chorus
marches chanting down your back to burn.

With such pain,
such pride,

the chorus bellows louder,
like a vast ox, louder, until

you yawn open,
maw this gift, and seal.

Still from the silence faintly spill—
or seem to spill—strains
of you, dearest lex, *regia sed militans.*

Lux Aeterna

You extend the offer of yourself:
unbroken and uninflected light
falling on the glass ocean forever.

You make room for the single voice,
a chamber in the hall of light
that glitters on the swaying sea.

You extend the offer of yourself,
you welcome me into your hall
then you end, and drain away,
like the wall at the end of the ocean.

Dream of the Hunt

I came across
a not quite pond
off the fence trail.

Drowned trees stood
or leaned together
like broken teeth.

Under the dusk
the surface
of the pond shone black.

I climbed in,
drawing the water
across me like a cloak.

Helplessly Baroque, My Soul

Twenty days,
three weeks, and it would vanish,
or I would, from it—I felt
a tearing
in my chest
as each day passed
through me—can I hold on
to this room another month, will some money
trickle through?

Some ideas came to me,
but they were bad;
my nerves tightened

as I rustled through the apartment
I knew I would lose, fingertips
lingering on
my books, the bright little implements

I had bought for the kitchenette,
my mother's face,
my copper vase.

The walls of that room had become my skin.

Imagine how long I paused, how stupid
I felt when I had to pause with a soft
potato in my left hand, a peeler in my right,
until I could plant its ploughsharish blade
firmly in that flesh beginning to
nurture eyes, until I could
slide it toward me.

After money came or before—
the difference to me!
but I can't remember—
I crept up to my hole after drinking,
undid bolt, lock, entered, blinked:
all my windows trembled.

It became slowly clear the two-room
above me was blasting the *Eroica*.
—I put my palm to a pane, the glass slab
throbbed like the heart of a deer
then was still, then throbbed.

I dropped my hand, sat cross-legged, and looked up.

I hoped that apartment was full of friends
nestling together or sprawled on the floor
with cups of cheap merlot, and some
had closed their eyes for the funeral march
and were humming along like me.

If We Are to Go Forward

Don't let your shoulders wilt as you sit at the table
sinking your head into the flowers
you snipped and fed.

Don't cry because you wound up in this room
as this fragile little person. Even you
saw, or heard, or sensed
moments of choice
walking past.

Don't cry, not even silently. If the wetness
should rot the lilies' smooth faces
so soon, if they should shut
and bloom inward again,
where would you turn?

Or if like a herd they should sense your breath
among them, if they should begin to quiver
and circle, and glow, faint at first
then unbearable, twenty
wan suns flaring

Absurdly in the gloom above you, all around you, no matter
where you turn in the frigid wood,
your slender heart thrashing,
your eyes dead in the glare,
then who, then what
have you become?

II

Alterations

A Bought Scene

He was a playwright busking that in New Orleans.
So I was the Girl with Tragedy in her Past.

Look on how the poor live and be glad,
or weep, he whispered into my ear's cave.

I wept for him: his neck was so spare,
just a tube with speech inside, that I wrapped
my scarlet scarf around it.
                              Wolfishly he watched me.

Or he would point questions: Was speaking
as hard for me as it was for him?
I had hurt; but had I hurt enough to speak?

This last he mused in a cruelly even voice
as I rode him: he refused to move with me
and instead pinched hard the inside
of my upper arm, then my ass, my full breast.

We awoke very near the river of a Sunday noon,
two corpses tapestried on the levee's ripple side.

He yawned, scratched, spit out a tooth.
He tongued with mild curiosity the hole, then said
"I've been thinking I should publish."
And though I was ready to, and soon did,
I tell you I was pained to leave.

The Deep Tourist

pays through his nose
for the comforts he enjoys.
He takes his tea white
at Sherwood's, then
a wee excursion
to the Dwarfie Stane
of Hoy.
            Not much to say.

So easy to forget,
genial, diminutive, rich.
            "Rich."

What is he collecting?
At Saqqara, he

bribes the guard and guide
(who wears a robe)
to buy the privilege
of descending the angled
            tight shaft
to the queen's chamber.

Fifty feet beneath flint dunes
in the thalamus,
he finds it cool, close.
With piano fingers
he traces
            the wall:

one carved cartouche repeats
her name. With his tongue,
the tourist tests

the dew gathered
on his fingertip.
Salt.

Catch him before sunset,
he's least reserved: he loves
photography
in the old way:
so is looking down
into the light meter
he's looped casually
around his neck.

"The golden hour."

Two strays doze in the heat,
a local drinks from the bottle.
On the wharf, the Punta Flaca,
the tourist is just past them all.
Tripodded, looking out, he awaits
the shot he's prepared for:

flying fish lifting
silver from the glass
bahía. At dusk these calm waters
can glow, you see,
like an eye.

My M.V.

A short man pyramids rocky avocados
as, passing in smooth black,
pale millionaires swill Starbucks.
Even the dead streets throb
like fat vein, beneath your heels,
and *are themselves* . . .

I hate that I can't love New York.
                      So I cruise
an Aegean for
boredom, boredom, come home

until ensemble in June we summer—
                      and a vast Adirondack
    day
drifts overhead like cold lake, the archaic spruce
shudder.
          (Mark my stoic indifference.)
                         Friends
are devastating clay birds in the pasture:
Pop. Pop. On the pond, with the gorgeous boat,
others trace an eyebrow.
                        Fucking *Listen*
    just once: I found
soloing, on your silk and milky flank, to yield
pleasure so sharp I cried
                as it bit its way out of my chest.

Let me watch as you wash off. You have to know
as well as I the weight of the mood that afterward
breathes,
and bears down
                        as mindless sunlight golds the oaken
        furniture.

                                        Then the sky is red
        and black,
a fling of stars burns directly overhead, jewel ghosts, and
        St. Jerome

spreads his hands: in the middle
of the current, not of it, look,
                                        our city
smolders on its crag like the cormorant.
                                        Stare
into the liquid image: there
is the hold broken:
we flicker past.

The Problem Bear

Out with a deputy,
I killed it.
    A dry and brittle
summer in Colorado.

We heaved it on the back
of the quad and roped it down
and all three of us tore
along the logging road to town.

It seeped. They didn't want it
at the station, but the corpse was fine
for dogs. My friend the science teacher
brought her summer kids.

It wasn't till we sawed the head
off and peeled away the pelt
that it became my body spread
on the steel table, my muscles dark
under a clear blue membrane, fist
sized pockets of fat.

Someone squeezed the urine out,
ripped the gall bladder. The colon
caved wetly between my fingers.
Slowly, some of the stench faded.

But it took me straddling
the carcass and smashing down the raised ax
to break open the ribcage—

I seemed to walk through a door.

Puffy, mottled black, the heart
slithered from my hand.

Well into the fall, the dogs
ate well, and were happy.

Quad

A winter lightlessness so perfuse
on the paths of the common
and around its stricken fountain
as in my four rooms, that despite
a handful of good days
darkness drifted in through
the cracks in my lips
and lodged at the bottom of my heart,
where jagged ice crystals unfolded.

Whenever I became aware of the muscle, sharp pain.
When a band of cardinals attacked the dormant
hazels, and perched in the holly, and whistled,
stupid with life, I was grieved, and sought
to understand, and buried myself in Chaucer.

These were the shrouds that April had to creep through.
It crept through: so much
desire crackled in me that my mind seemed broken
into smaller, warring minds.
I got into the car.
                      Clear weather meant
undergrads milling half-nude everywhere.
A faint shock—but then
these beings of the flesh
seemed each to house a ghost of me—

Between black, bare oaks, a football
player wound up extravagantly and lofted
a football. It rose high in a lazy arc
and fell too steeply for the girl to catch.
She scolded, but she might have been impressed,
or too busy playing playful to care.

I sat in the chapel's cool shadow
because the benches in the sun were taken.
Yet I felt I had a room to myself, a window
to watch these gorgeous, ardent people
in pairs, flocks, or alone, entangle
and brush and look aloof and watch,

as I did, the football flowing back and forth
with frequent mishaps.
                          Then it slowed
at an apex, where I perceived

that only a yard above, and to the right,
in the bright air between branches,
a pale hawk with three red streaks on his breast,
not huge, but large, scanning, hung.

Child in the Yard

Towards you who once sowed beneath the wall these
    staggered green
banks of bamboo and osier, reed, and often working stopped
    to lean
sightless of me on a granite fence-pillar of your own hewing,
    craning your neck back
to hear more purely lithe stalks slithering against each other,
    sad Jacques,
your pond going *pulse* and *pulse* against a berm
equally cut by you, while atop it thickened the fleshy film
of lilies and purple-fringed floating hearts—that as the level
    fluxed breathed
weakly—I just look at you, at ease amid the terrors of your
    labor and modest wealth
until your calvinized eyes crack open, and the black cores of
    them range
together up this fat calf, my pair of crimson shorts, over this
    strange
brachycephalic skull in whose hallow misshapen chambers
    I—the deep I—twirl
languid as the throttled Isadora, while from my blubbery lips
    spray pearls
of spittle; or perhaps I squat monk-quiet in that cavern, alone
    and aching to match
an outer to my inner world, but how could you ever catch
the difference—toward you I will take nine strong steps

then nine steps back, because you have died, and your
     strength rips
at the stiffening fabrics of me even in breaking down
its own memory into free elements, as surely I have shown.

Thou in Time

With the mower passing over
the lawn this August morning

shirtless, lightheaded

it is such easy going, you just
push it along and the fresh swathe
follows after, good machine,

and what Mother called the smell of *order*
wafts up from the headless
plants

      around you, around you—

and who has no excuse like you, none?
You cry quietly, birdsong
occurring here and there, as you observe
the sun sinking
into the torn trunks

of trees . . . numbed on the porch
beneath the yellow porch light, you let
mosquitoes settle on your forearms, chest, and throat
and drink deep
motionless, by the hundred

then you rub yourself, and cherry juice—

Please take pity,
speak to me,
come inside.

Look—
I am drinking the rose, now
I drink the thorns.

The Derelict

Down the stair in slant sun,
to Washington Park, where he sits.

The iron fence leans like a shadow
into the park; and it throws its shadow.

A rusted gate at each corner, and all agape.

You will say to yourself, who are these souls
towing their dogs, their maimed guitars?

Drifting out, drifting in—

It is such a little patch of earth, and so threadbare,
worth nobody's time.

Nor can you see
with the sun blasting in, so low and molten—

let it go.

These are good servants—they only wait,
or sing now and then, or laugh, or fall asleep.

He watches them fall asleep. In the air
above them, a mist of gnats; farther,

a tiny, glinting jet plows east, opening
two blood-colored furrows.

III

Ab Ovo

A Beginning

One night the wind heaves down the nest
and places it on the street.
Then morning makes altars everywhere.

Recovering it,
mind the bright shards enfolded there,
the snapped fishing line.

Mind the scene as it was
when you saw it first:

The almond tree was flowering
over soaked pavement
daubed red.

The world was still, and it held
a measure of emptiness.

The Tines

My father threw his weight into the helve
and sunk a pitchfork in the mound
of old straw—the tang of rot—my body
was so thin, the muscles were mere
ideas, tender, beautiful, and I thought the tines
of the tool were beautiful too—standing in a dim barn
that the weather roamed through I was stunned
by a reverence for the edges men
wielded, shears, mowers, for the straight lines
they spoke between them, working so steadily, an ache,
because whenever I opened my mouth to speak,
even something trivial, *I'm tired,*
I'd like to go home, the world stormed in—
stammering beneath gray eyes, my face broken,
crying—every muscle of my father's back gathered
as again he lifted, an enormous load, but I
couldn't watch him,
I was trying to be
the three tines
that poked through, long, curving up,
as they caught the pale light
and gleamed, as my father staggered
toward the white noon and the wheelbarrow.

Milkweed

The summer morning,
the exploding front, the rain
a wall falling—

glass, the skylight aches;
bitter thunder grinds;
and the thin leaves,
the tender skin
of the clearing,

shake in seizure—

One stalk of milkweed
jerks left and right, is twisted
down, blown
upright, bitten, blind thing, on and on,
by the swarm of bullets:
then in the lull
it sways.

In its pods,
molecule by molecule, smoke-
colored silk
thickens,

the only food
of the monarchs,
wandering rags.

Our City Center

By that trait of time she called
idiopathy we could almost
console each other: how
it occurs, despite us,
fresh—our days were short,
it was fall, and the afternoons
a hell of light, except when a storm sailed
overhead, drenching Havana.
                              She had to clerk
on summons, wear the vermilion blouse
and cream pants. Where I had nothing
to do.
        Fruits were: guava, avocado, pineapple.
And in beige heaps, yucca. All bore
the impasse of invitation.
We owed our plenty to the city's
fragmentary garden districts—

And I had no friends among the émigrés,
loathing our resemblances, and each language
we could converse in seemed to me,
because of just that, obsolete—
                              she shifted up
on her hip and elbow, in bed—*¿Y ya?*
she asked, because I was leaving today.
Her skin was so white

they harried her, and she glowed
in the first threads of light.
Hungrily

a bird screamed from the window sill,
green, with a blaze of ivory on its throat.

Barcelona: Implication

The Constellations are a harmoniously
composed series of 23 gouaches that Miró
painted to escape the trauma of the war
years.

—Fundació Joan Miró

We've all gouached.
Haven't we? Pollock lashed
stretched canvas that was Nude.
Was said to call his Ruth prude
and he spat chew in a coffee can
and shat bloodily in the can.

When I was twenty I spent three
hours in a room with the Free-
Spirited types moving from
one inviting orifice to the welcome
of another. I was lost in my wood,
savage, and stern. But also I understood
that when it was later and I was wiser
I could never forgive Herr Pfizer.

My father said we've all got an East River.
He had a tenuous web of veins for a liver.
His loss. Literally. Mom's impatient art
was proved to be the most effective part
of her mothering: you should see her rich greens
well up in the power of the middle and grow lean
as they colonize the crusted edges.
My love for her is impregnable.

Pity Miró, moonblind, weary on the rocky coast
of Portugal, walking cliff paths and getting lost.
His quest for childish wonder has bent him
and riddled his skin before its time.
Put this together with that! Paint it yellow!
Murk the sky with banks of Periwinkle and Snow.
Gouache a widened eye low on the right,
so it can behold the left and the night.

In the Cloisters

She sticks out
very little
from her midnight robe:
round head, a hand.

Her expression is as blessed
as a mannequin's.
She has almost no palm

and it faces me:
in its folds three
short, scratched lines
almost connect.

From it, five
long fingers rise
like smoke. "Stop,"
or, "Please, stop."

New York

A Problematic Relationship

We unlock
the top and bottom locks
of the apartment door and sink into chairs. Now—
now we can be nothing more
than a web between the nouns we care for.

But one evening we discovered
a red-kerchiefed basket on the step
heaped high with storms like blue potatoes.
The note beneath the basket read, "Thinking of you
—Fall," in hieroglyphics.

I find myself speaking for you. Whereas together
do we talk at all?
                    Each morning I go watch the sun
struggle up from under the river.

Runners dodge around me, so lithe
the air barely stirs.

Webs of red light spreading over the river:
how can I grasp the force of that current
until the wind begins to push against it
and a fierce chop begins there between piles
of the bridge, an agon—

You are paler than you know when you first wake up,
but stately and firm-thighed, bending over the basin
with its horsehair glaze,
                        and there's a voice on the radio,
a singer of our parents' generation.

How slowly you pivot,
turning on me that eye that
before coffee is a whale's eye,
closing, worldless.

Then the Animals Move Slowly

The month spent reading Spenser in a cabin
on a hill above the ocean on the northern edge
of Nova Scotia as a nation of winds gathered
down on the gray waves, and muttered to each other
and screamed at each other until they made
common purpose: on the middle day of November
they came against my bluff, and winter began.

IV

Mosaic of a Dog in Crete

Town by town, west to east,
they conceded the island,
the Byzantines, though control
lingered around Gortyn,
commanding a good valley,
a center for their culture
of grains, olives, and citrus.
Late pottery attests to trade, if
modest. One temple-
cum-storehouse reveals a frieze
of Ceres in an enviable
state of preservation.

Thirty-five kilometers distant,
at the mouth of a south-facing
sea valley find Lissos, once
another prized conquest.
—Not so lucky, this. Its valley
a gulch, narrow, not fertile,
the city's virtue was priority:
lived in so long
before the Romans expanded, the sandstone
of its western wall already
porous with cubby graves.

Graceful, their half-and-half system:
the dead get the west bank and the living
the east. Daily your sunlight starts
and endures an hour after theirs.
As I hinted, there's nothing left
in that gorge given over to oak
and someone's ravenous, sleepy goats.
Hundreds of shadowy holes to your left,
crumbling low walls in the center
of dubious antiquity. I did come across
a slavering dog pieced together
of black tesserae on a brambled
court up to my right—
to wit, the living half—and I felt
a distasteful superiority
as I stood above him there.

Holt Hill

Its name will no longer work: meaning I think *woodlot*
in Saxon, and so one effect of the coming felling
of its softwood timber—a task the preservation
society undertook, to restore the meadows and open

the prospect to Boston—will be the further spreading
of a place-name rift.
                            But still, like sinew, trails wind
beneath hushed pines. From the clouds that have pressed
the state all afternoon a violet-orange evening drops.

And at the top, I've caught it, sprawled
in a clearing beside the concrete sphere,
a fire reservoir of the twentieth century,
as the world's color fades.

As the Prudential Tower
twinkles on, a pale green inch.

Helsingør

The Øre ripples brightly around
Elsinore's shelf of sand.
I circled its dark walls twice
in pearl light
because the drawbridge was raised.

What did I gain? Between the water
of the sound and the battlements
a row of anglers
rocked back, reached forward
whipping their rods, each cast—
rhythmic as the breakers into which
they dropped the high-test lines.
Is that water still rich? Do swirling currents help?
I don't know.
Some left, others came.

What did I gain? It was as if I'd tasted
a crude antidepressant:
the smatter of salty rocks,
sea, sun, and my black
texturous woolens all radiated
a *contentment*
that even in the moment I felt
was unearned, thin as tissue,
and utterly desirable.

Was this flittering sense—
I call it happiness—
sufficient recompense
for the closed portcullis,
or the reason the castle was barred?

No, I owe that to not knowing
the winter hours.

Others told me what's inside.
"It's more effete than I would have liked,"
my mother said, "but I liked it." "It's got nothing
on the play"—my father.
"A tourist trap. Watch out."

I stared at length, though from a distance,
at the protuberant lips of gargoyles
that drained its corner church—much

pitted by the sulfurous rains.
I saw the aspiration in those greening copper spires,
the work that went into grandiloquent stonework.
I see no need to come back here in my life.
Still, I had planned a day around this.

My mind seems a function of what I've seen, and when:
a ponderous collection of whimsical lenses,
each wrested painfully. Is anything I think
inexplicable? I know my loneliness
has been built from others': is it still mine?

Before I strolled away from the grounds
to find breakfast by the defunct dry dock—
now this dead shipbuilding town's
"Harbor of Culture"—
I indulged in a longing gaze.
Spiked cannons bristled from the outworks,
and were reflected in the weedy moat beneath.
There was a swan floating on that rank water,
big, grayish, and, it seemed, headless.
She was motionless for so long I thought she had drowned.
But then she reared up her muscled neck
and looked sternly left and right,
beak parted,
her head dripping with oozy stalks.

Wavering, Changing

All around itself the crepe myrtle unfolds
ten thousand leaves simultaneously.

That *pain:* each blade slicing
out through the stiff vein
                          for a week. And crowds, as now

ponderous Arab governments are toppling left
then right.

              My ancestors are seeping
from their graves;
                      the gods of cause, the gods
of effect, scrap in the shadows;
                              hot blood
floods my lips, my fingertips—a prickling—

                  Two destroyers, a trireme, a brigantine,
lost, sea anchor in darkness:
they let out gossamer ten miles long,
wind comes, the cords foul, the hulls shiver together,
black tonnages, grinding, grinding, and the ribs
open, men breathe ocean—

                          Our shadows
fall on the esplanade.
Evening, you murmur to the passersby.

Two promenading citizens.

Your sunglasses glint red, you secure them
in the massed coils of your hair. Overhead

the window of a condominium
is drawn up.
                    In my back,
the nerve tree tightens its roots.

I can sense the razed temple, it must be near.
Weren't we made to wander on?
Weren't we told to roof it well?

Resort Town

You stand,
searching the small, bright waves
for an hour,

then sit on the bench,
rigid, soundless
under the tear and sigh
of the surf,

until you are lying on the stone
of the seawall,
your face pointed at the sun,
the wind moving in your hair,
your chest now rising,
now falling.

Flood

Roofs yawn open
to the sky, which is smooth,
silky, hot and a weak
blue again.

The crown
of the oak bows
into the water.

Pouring from a hole
in the center of the sky
light flattens
onto motionless water.
The light presses
rungs of cloud
into the mirror.

My boat drifts over a house.

The sky darkens,
the flood darkens.

Ten yards off

a little splash—
the moon floats
from the water,
round, dripping.

Thick glow
fills the boat
to its gunwales,

and the boat
sinks slowly

to the house—

Enduring Pleasures

Into me
a child broke
out of me

at Lent.

At five
on Tuesday
the sky darkens
like a brick
in the fire.

✻

On the swan float, paused,
men in masks—heart-shaped
black, sequin-spangled—
scream for tits,
dangle fistfuls of gold
and purple beads.

The drooping Hoosier
beside me lurches
into the street
and flaps out his.
They rain on him.

A jeune brunette
haggles up.
What do I get
for a snatch?

❋

Sadness rushes you
from the corner of your eye—

You stagger back,
miséricordieux, miserably
self-aware,
but grin and go on
for others, mostly—

So stroll down this sidestreet
twelve hours earlier:

Prytania: azaleas bloom,
candle flames of color
and scent flickering on
two hundred twigs—

You're content, so thin in the air,
but still (*why?*) want to pry
open the sticky furls—

Endymion, Rex,
Bacchus, Zulu,
Tucks, Muses.

❋

Friday night I am two-stepping with Lucy.
I remember—lovely.

Joan is swung in the arms of someone large,
winking at everybody the while.

Suzanne is on the prowl,
stumbling into people, on the prowl.

Parker stirs his Old Fashioned at the bar.
He sends affectionate messages to New York.

Will is two streets down, he claims via text,
getting, hahahaha, a dance from Cherry.

        ✳

Cigars of a morning,
a Connecticut broadleaf wrapper
with Nicaraguan filler, oaky and rather mild,
over the second
and speculative cup of coffee.

"Speculum."

I am across the table from my childhood
influences: we chat, construe
our shred of common ground.

Will talks of money.
He wants it. His fiancée is still
in the picture.
I smoke softly, and wonder

how many welts
we raised
on each other's skin
with paintballs.

✳

Parker, hell, of course I'm hung over. But
hey, I *like* the feeling—at least
I once did: that counts.

(This talk unfolds Saturday, in the park
stilled with swans with dark
shadows on the grass.)

It's just—when I swing my head too fast
now to look at *x,* it doesn't work,
and I swim in black

for a second. Afterward it's like I see seams
where the nouns are stitched together,
they break open at the corners:

the swans, say.
A brightness spills out.

He ribs me. We both know I'm full of shit.

✳

Everyone is here—
at least one guest from each of my lives.
So I mediate,
living between them.

Hugh Laurie is the King of Bacchus;
with a cane, he resurrects House for the mob.
Quentin Tarantino is said to seem
"fleshy and constipated." My set
agrees he's never been an actor.

We're sure all the Saints are here:
one aboard the Navy's papier-mâché destroyer,
one on the half shell: a Venus float.
They pump their fists and hurl lamé footballs
past the balconies. We go wild.

Pygmalion, Choctaw,
Druids, Cleopatra, Nyx,
Babylon, Chaos,
Orpheus, Morpheus.

❋

Lucy is often with me.
I am often with Lucy.

Light is brilliant in the dark.

                              At noon,
darkness glows everywhere.

❋

Enter flambeaux to the tune of hautboys,

Spangle macadam with laminate doubloons

To glint back as the black-clad troop tramps

Past hoisting hissing propane torches and flame.

Fade out oboes; swell slowly the drum and tuba

Under the shrill and pealing-out spears of trumpets.

The marchionettes that follow are pre-pubertal

Distracted and in from other states. They twirl.

❋

To think I had desired
from this act
a kind of translation—

some rekeying—

néanmoins, la voici—
afloat in the air,
another failed evasion.

❋

We return to a room:
the cut lilies
have fallen apart
on the dining table.

Your little smile is back.
Dead tired, still we . . .

A kind of love is being
built.
                    Later
with our plastic riches in your hands,
you gaze up
at the bead tree.

Automatic Pool Cleaner

Like the stubborn rover *Spirit,* it's
insistent in collecting its units
of grime, if less scientific. Like a white ray
it cruises slowly through teal.
It's someone's leashed flounder, or
a menace that has come too close
to the surface and now spurts
from his tail a warm cupful
that misses my leather sandals.

Look at him go. Ingeniously
independent, he's replaced
the pool boy, whose dim ghost
imbues him with comic eros
and just a nibble of pathos.

But as he tries to force a way
into the shallows, where scalloped steps
march down—rise up—
he becomes bewildered. His flagellum
lashes sadly forth and back.
I haul him up and turn
him toward the deeper center.

Faithful as a Labrador
he scoots away on his errand
and his wake laps my ankles:
isn't everything real entirely real?

Plastic shoes, plastic chair, so what;
I too have been known
to ceaselessly pace a little cell.

The lawn, fertilized, gasps
weakly in the dense heat as it grows.
Yellow as cake, an inner tube
drifts over the snarl
of the machine's umbilical.

It's Tuesday at three. Friends of mine
are off in offices, classrooms, labs, Brazil,
or the Bay creating wealth,
girding for a future they pursue.

But their acquaintance sips icy coffee
in his latest attempt to fire
his forebrain to a lyre: some thing
he can hold and have, that returns
more life than it burns, a thing
gorgeous, worthless, and self-betraying.

O sun on water, O sun on matter.
Kiss my limbs, my lips as I recline away
into this, the prime of my decay.

Empathy

I was the tree all afternoon,
drawing my life from the air.

Thrushes' grace made me haunt of music.
Light streamed into me and was woven

into a gold-green tapestry
that I unmade, made, and laid

to abandon on the golden grass.
When the sun dragged the last light

back into himself, I sighed,
but did not lower my worshipful arms.

✳

Tonight I see you are the sky,
pierced by a million diamond nails,

your children, that may be dead.
Into nothingness, into me

the light escapes its birth—
but you are torn

and vast, all hide.
The zone of deepest black,

the most riddled, is your heart:
it stretches to your very edge

which now glows wan,
now crumbles away to bluish ash.

❋

Morning

I study to live my death well.
Through the chilly forest,

my mind ravens on ahead
of my life

like a silent, monstrous bulldozer
chased by a chariot with bells.

On the Levee

Fat, tame, turbid,
the river ripples brightly.
Upstream the rain
droned on,
so these willows are sunk
neck-deep
and chunks of dirt are torn
from the bank.

The infrastructure holds:
the crest has passed.

This is accommodation.

❋

In another month I begin
to teach again. I remember the *Ethics*
when I can't fall back to sleep,
then over pho with my sister
as she dissects her breakup,
her demi banh-mi.

A year since I worked.
I don't think I am worse,
but have determined that I can't know.
A post-Catholic remorse
lingers: aftertaste.

Whenever I regard my past
at middle distance—
specifically, the little, grandiloquent myths
I nurtured and (saving grace) hid—
my perception, thus judgment,
darkens to an irony so dense
it admits no freer hatch.

I hate that I can't get past the dreadful
naïveté of those selves, can't forgive them
their bundles of earnest expectation,
their stubborn attempts to distill
the quotidian into *meaning.*

Poor things, proud as Huck,
drifting downriver,
getting smaller.

❋

At twenty-two I wanted to see purely.
(I knew less and less, even then, what that meant.)
But by exertion or hunger
or sex or abject failure
I could arrive at a state in which my body
was hollowed out, leaving
a skin which lived
and seemed to see.

I wanted not to need other people:
I needed a platform that I would build
from my experience, my silence.

Chasing that,
I neared Cathedral Mountain—
its gloomy strata
loomed above the clearing
spotted with house-sized erratics,
past the icebound saddle
and the arête.

Slowly, the forests I loved
resisted me. The rock flared white
in the sun, and that blankness spread through my mind.

Tore through it.

Now I can remember just
laboring through deadfall, a sourceless
smoke smell, fistfuls of ibuprofen.

And I remember when an August storm strewed
my gear a mile down the bed
of Joseph Canyon.

I saw the lack
rising toward me
through the surface of each thing—
I turned.

✳

Whatever logic shadows
this form of thinking forces me
to claim for the present,

if not triumphant synthesis,
the growth of knowledge—

But uncertainty is my new way,
it was found, then sought,
and now on a weekday afternoon
I can lounge by a river in mild flood
failing to identify the intermittently hidden
and fast-passing fragments of flotsam.

✳

I came here, and sensation
for three months
held me up—

the fan-palm striped the blue stucco wall
in a chilly afternoon
which continued
until suddenly wet warmth filled the wind,
the Japanese magnolias popped big magenta
fists on their bare branches
and the thrushes were floating back and forth
across the city, at the center
of their piercing cryings-out—

Even when my moods came over me,
when I had to huddle over a desk
and work desperately at thought,
at that proving,
there was still enough of it
in me to sustain me. Elsewhere
too, winter held.

✳

But as that ebbed the person I had made
and worked to make for twenty-four years
resurfaced: the self-impatience
that bled over onto others,
the useful guilt,
and its black, corrosive parent.

I fought it: I wanted
to save this new uselessness,
to make it useful—
to make it *moral.*

(Such an awkward, powerful word—I write it
in the hope that after long labor
I may be able to justify
that part of my life to me.)

✳

Carnival built, struck, faded—
It was an afternoon in March.

I walked streets, then the louche park.
It flowered madly.
Braced on my roof in the sun, I read a novel,
then came down and fell into the daybed—

I can discover no line between my dreams. There
I am often a rain of glass
tinkling on the cobbles. Flanked by tugs and a pilot boat,
I am a laden tanker

creaking down the Mississippi's
final sigmas,
and I think I am the flood itself—

I awoke in unexpected dark.
I began to walk—
night began to end, which meant

that in loose bands the disappointed
bachelors were marching home
through the Quarter.

Good evening, one said.
Good morning, I said, heavily—

my sadness was absolute.

I could smell the early jasmine
blooming on both sides of Royal Street,
and I could see, beneath its tangle, the wrought iron screens
gorgeously excluding,
the jagged glass that topped a wall.

❊

This, though, is the levee.
When wind fans the willows' leaves
they whisper.

Then the breeze abates, leaving an enormous silence,
the silence in which the river lives. Jealously

I conceive of its power—

and I remember my house at my back,
three blocks,
a cheery pastel purple.

The crest has passed into the Gulf.

❖

I will be meeting children, charming parents.
I will take shelter
in the world's idea
of worth.

I need to save this year,
I will need to return here.

                           So lightly,
in this indolent heat,

I let myself break
the word that sticks: *de, cadence.*

If my life is sad rich music,
very well—
may it fall upon the ear
drop by drop.

If I am tumbling from a high place,
may it last.

River Path

I slow, I
            stop: they surround me.

Lights
        rising together from this field
                            in dark Connecticut,

this roughly mown
this humid field

at dusk, creeping out from under
                            the fat, chopped stalks
strewn in wakes to dry and not drying,
                            as a pall
of rose, threads of smoke
fade through the sky, the long liquid

                            day is collapsing

everywhere,
and everywhere now,
                the fireflies
                            in their plated suits
in silence,
in midair

            gather
the force of their small lives and burst
into pale flame

for one half-second, the animal
is consumed,
dissolved,

then, near, a carapace glows—

Night wind fingers the fringe of maples and black gums,

pulls each leaf back, the dark silver.

I catch my breath and I am invisible;
my bare head is an eye.
                                          On
and off,
          this sparkling matrix of pinpricks,

instant death and instant life,
fills the air entirely,
from the damp grasses up through the canopy,
further—

and my heart is not beating, and I know
they are each one identical, each one screaming
the same need in the same way with one intent,
screaming soundlessly for each other—

How patiently they flicker off
and on, silent, silent, composing
around me the saddest brain in the world,
the stupidest, the thinnest.
                                          It fades,

it grinds west, it chases the twilight.

Across from the Winter Palace

Do you remember when you began to travel?
It lent you this astonishing lens and you kept a journal
that rode in your breast pocket like a stone.
There you wrote "Limoges—" and "ALTENKIRCHEN"
and when you kissed, saw a *peasant*, or passed out—
died for twenty seconds—in the heat on the hill above
Marseille you would rush out the notebook and make
    a note—
sometimes just an x in the top right corner—
and ideally you would brood about that later.

Which led slowly to the dark hot bar
where you enjoy a glass of beer across from the Winter Palace
    in summer.
In the rose-and-blue windows of the basilica
today radiant burghers stood and learned Mercy in a circle
around Stephen, recognized
by the pebble enthroned in his skull and the scarlet ooze.

While in your system the amphetamines progress.
The idea is they'll give you heart to haul yourself up and
    cross
the limestone plaza. And when at the gate of the place
you pay you can enter the Palace.

Acknowledgments

I thank the editors of the following publications, where these poems first appeared, sometimes in different form:

The Adroit Journal: "On the Levee," "La Dolce Vita," "Wavering, Changing"
AGNI: "Automatic Pool Cleaner," "Helsingør"
American Poets: "Thou in Time"
BOAAT: "The Tines"
The Missouri Review: "Milkweed," "Flood," "If We Are to Go Forward," "River Path"
PHANTOM: "The Deep Tourist"
Poetry: "Barcelona: Implication," "Across from the Winter Palace"
PRØOF: "Two Apostrophes to the Requiem"
Prodigal: "Enduring Pleasures"
The Southern Review: "A Problematic Relationship" (as "Little Sails")
Two Peach: "Dream of the Hunt," "Helplessly Baroque, My Soul"
The Yale Review: "Thereafter," "Like the Pelican"

✳

I am indebted everywhere I look. Though this list can only be partial, I bow here to those teachers who shaped me: Louise Glück, Rosanna Warren, Harold Bloom. Many read and responded to poems in this book, including Chiara Scully, Rodger Kamenetz, Max Ritvo, Hannah Loeb, Rebecca Dinerstein, David Ferry, and Jordan Zandi: I thank them. Adelaide Russo was a faithful friend as this book came together: merci.

Carl Phillips, glimpsing fire in this book, made that fire real. I thank him profoundly for his judgment, his kindness, his vision.